The Koroua and the Mauri Stone

Text and illustrations
ROBYN KAHUKIWA

I tipu te mauri, te mauri nui,
te mauri roa, te mauri whakaea,
ki te whai ao, ki te ao mārama.
Tihei mauriora!

PUFFIN BOOKS

Once there was a koroua who spent many of his days sitting on his porch looking at the land where his ancestors had lived and died.

The world was so different now. Even when he was a boy, Papa-tū-ā-Nuku had been covered with trees: Miro, Karaka, Matai, Tawa, Pūriri, Kōtukutuku, Tōtara, Ponga, Tī Kouka, Rimu and Kaikōmako.

And the birds, there had been so many birds of different kinds: Tūī, Kākāriki, Tīwaiwaka, Kererū, Ruru, Kotare, Tauhou, Riroriro, Korimako, Kōkako, Kiwi and Pīpīwharauroa.

The mauri had still been strong then, the life force still strong from the time when Tāne Mahuta had placed his children, the trees, the birds, the lizards, the insects, on the body of his mother Papa-tū-ā-Nuku.

There had been a mauri stone in the forest, hidden long, long ago under the roots of a Tōtara tree known only to his ancestors.

The koroua could remember the old people talking about it. He did not know where it was or what had become of it. Nobody did.

The mauri stone of Tāne's children had been lost, and without it their life force would not be protected. The trees, birds, lizards and insects had gone.

Now there was nothing to look at but grass, nothing to listen to but sheep. And, more than anything else, the koroua longed for the birds to come back.

One day, he decided what he would do. He would make a kite, a kite made in the tradition of his ancestors, a kite to find the mauri stone of Tāne's children.

It would be shaped like a bird to remind him of the birds that had once lived there.

It took the koroua all winter to make his kite.

When it was finished, he named his kite Kāhau. Afterwards he called his family so they could see it. The large bird kite was impressive. It was made from toetoe and mānuka, covered with a weaving of harakeke and hung with bunches of feathers. On the face of the cloth was a finely painted moko and paua shell eyes that glowed. Hanging down between the legs like a tail was the pūhihi — a long, multi-feathered plume — and an aho of twisted muka came from the puku of the bird.

'This kite has the mana, the ihi, the wehi,' a kuia said.

'What is it for?' a mokopuna asked.

The koroua replied, 'That is our bird to seek the mauri. I have made him for a special purpose. He is the one who will find the mauri stone of the children of Tāne. His name is Kāhau.

'Until that mauri stone is in its rightful place, we will have no trees or birds living with us again.

'Tomorrow at dawn, we will let Kāhau fly from the top of the hill behind the marae. It is time for his journey.'

The next morning, just before dawn, the people carried Kāhau to the top of the hill.

When everyone was together, the old man turned to the people and said, 'Take hold of Kāhau and lift him high into the air.' The people did as they were asked, they lifted the kite high, but there was no wind to fly the kite. The koroua picked up the aho of Kāhau and began to chant.

Then the wind, Tawhirimatea, came. He blew great gusts of his breath. One of the gusts lifted the kite up into the air. Kāhau began to fly.

Up and down, ducking and diving, this way and that, he flew on the breath of Tawhirimatea while the koroua chanted.

The aho tugged hard at the old man's hands as the kite soared and swooped.

How magnificent Kāhau looked as he flew in the early morning sky!

Suddenly, with one gigantic swoop, the kite pulled his aho from the old man's hands and flew away.

Everyone looked at the old man, 'E, koro, we have lost our taonga, Kāhau. The kite is lost!'

'No,' replied the koroua. 'He is not lost. He has begun his
search for the mauri stone. We must follow him.'
And the people murmured in amazement. Still, they trusted
their kaumatua and did not doubt his words.
So the koroua and the people followed Kāhau
as he soared above their heads, the paua shell eyes
bright in his painted face.
They walked up hills and down again,
always with the kite just ahead of them,
flying on the breath of Tawhirimatea,
his puhihi fluttering behind him
in the wind.
Finally, Kāhau disappeared over a rise.

Climbing to the top, the koroua and the people were just in time to see the kite sink to the earth and lie still. Just as suddenly as it had started, the wind stopped.

Kāhau lay on his back with his head and wings covered with water. He had come to rest on the edge of a dam made for the sheep.

The koroua picked up a stone that was lying in the water, near the head of Kāhau. He held the stone in both hands. 'Look,' he said, 'it is the mauri! We are given back the mauri stone of the trees, the birds, the lizards and the insects, the mauri stone of the children of Tāne. With this stone their life force will be protected so that once again they will live with us.'

And the people looked and saw that the stone the old man was holding was round and smooth with a hole in the middle, and carved into the top were two lizards, each biting the tail of the other.

'This is the mauri stone I heard the old people speak of,' said the koroua. 'Kāhau has found him.

'Now it is time for us to plant our trees, the many different trees that used to grow here on our land. The trees will provide food and shelter for the birds, lizards and insects. And we will place the mauri stone beneath the roots of the biggest Tōtara tree and wait for the birds to come back.'

MIRO

So the people planted Miro, Karaka, Matai, Tawa, Pūriri, Kōtukutuku, Tōtara, Ponga, Tī Kouka, Rimu and Kaikōmako. They planted seeds, seedlings, little trees and big trees.

Soon trees covered all the land as far as the eye could see, and the koroua and the people of his family took time caring for their trees.

They hid the mauri stone beneath the roots of the biggest Tōtara, and the old man made sure the young ones knew where it was so it would never be lost again.

Once more the koroua spent many of his days looking out at the land, but now he watched the trees growing, watched them getting bigger and stronger, and he smiled to himself.

And one day the birds came back!

Pages 4 and 5

1. Pūriri
2. Mamaku
3. Miro
4. Karaka
5. Tōtara
6. Ponga
7. Kaikōmako
8. Tawa
9. Kauri
10. Kōtukutuku
11. Nīkau
12. Tī Kouka
13. Patē
14. Karamū
15. Rangiora
16. Tī Kouka
17. Rimu
18. Matai
19. Kawakawa
20. Puahou
21. Harakeke
22. Karamū
23. Kōwhai

Pages 6 and 7

1. Ruru
2. Kōtare
3. Kererū
4. Korimako
5. Tauhou
6. Pīpīwharauroa
7. Kiwi
8. Kākāriki
9. Tīwaiwaka
10. Tūī
11. Kōkako
12. Riroriro

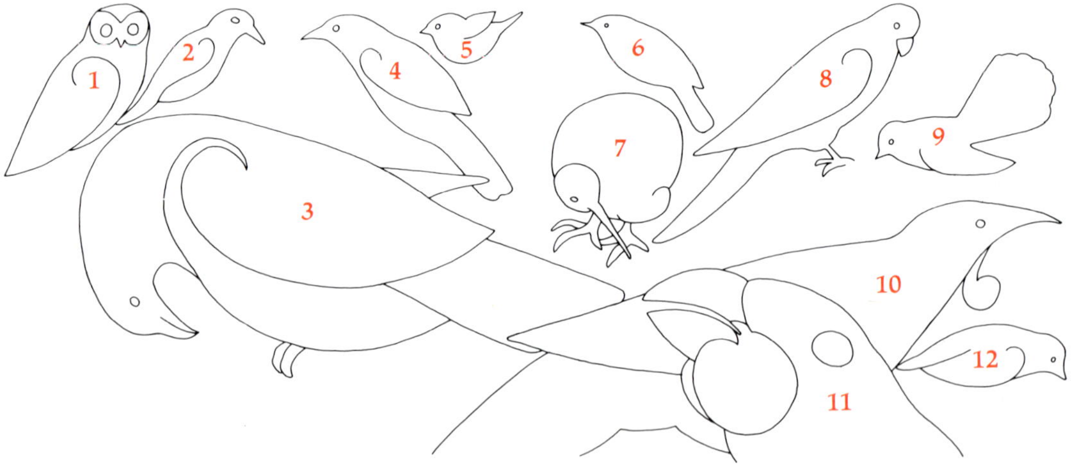

Pages 30 and 31

1. Kōtukutuku
2. Tī Kouka
3. Pīpīwharauroa
4. Korimako
5. Koekoeā
6. Kaikōmako
7. Kawakawa
8. Kaikōmako
9. Harakeke
10. Kiwi
11. Ruru
12. Rimu
13. Puahou
14. Tīwaiwaka
15. Tōtara
16. Ponga
17. Pūkeko
18. Kōtare
19. Kererū
20. Kahikatea
21. Mamaku
22. Ponga
23. Matai
24. Tauhou
25. Miro
26. Kōwhai
27. Tūī
28. Kaikōmako
29. Kōwhai

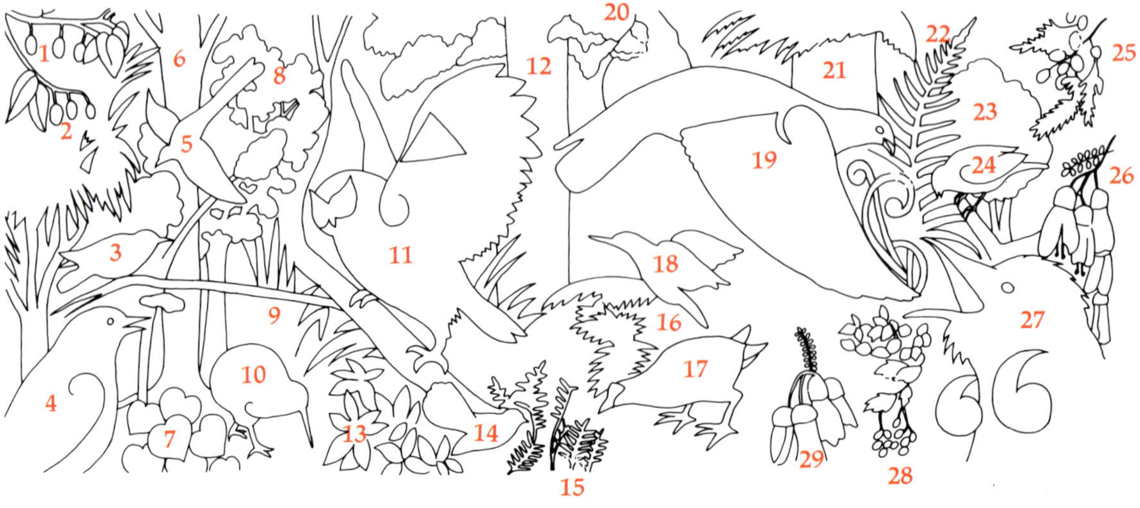